Hosanna, From a Traveller Behind the Sandstorm

Ana Hull

BookLeaf Publishing

India | USA | UK

Presentation by *BookLeaf Publishing*

Web: www.bookleafpub.com

E-mail: info@bookleafpub.com

ISBN: 9789363314696

First edition 2024

To my Father, for always being willing to play
"dead author" with me

ACKNOWLEDGEMENT

Firstly, thank you to the team at BookLeaf Publishing for creating this wonderful opportunity for myself and many other writers. I would also like to thank my family, and especially my parents, Eric and Michelle Hull, for their endless support and encouragement and countless sacrifices for my sake thus far, whether reading my very rough rough drafts or moving to an entirely different state for the sake of my education. Also thank you to my parents for showing me the movie Labyrinth as a child, since now I could not imagine sitting down to write without it on in the background. I would be remiss if I did not also take a moment to thank all of my friends who have supported me over the years. First, thank you to the Davis family for their encouragement in my writing, particularly my poetry. As well, thank you to Faith for finding this opportunity and sharing it with me, as well as for her support, encouragement, and kindness over the years. Thank you as well to Elaine for her continual friendship and for showing me what it means to truly be a goodhearted person. Finally, thank you to James, to whom no amount of gratitude is sufficient, for being such an incredible mentor and friend over the years, for being the reason I fell in love with philosophy (even if I am using that power to write poetry), for causing me to fall in love with learning, and for crucially altering the course of my life for the better. Thank you.

The Little Mud Men

How jealous I am of the little mud men.
They play their game perpetually
With peace secured in their haven
Of joy as frail as that peace may be.

They feel fragile to touch,
Yet seem to be at rest.
Though they do not own much
Of us two, they have it best.

They are frozen in a moment,
In a state of simplicity.
I am frozen in movement,
Wrought with worldly worry.

For all of time I wonder.
As old as time they seem.
I will always labor
While they live in a dream.

How jealous I am of the little mud men.
They have no responsibility.
Beautiful is the earth that made them then,
Though fragile just like me.

The Sorrowful Sun

In the early hours of the morn,
When most men are filled with scorn
And dread the day that lies ahead,
Weary, they still rest in their little bed.
They send curses to that blazing sun
Saying, "Oh devilish thing, why must you come
When in peaceful rest I could lay here?
But no, through that horrid window you must
peer!"
And the sorrowful sun, with a gentle gaze,
Pities the man whose eyes are glazed,
But bravely continues down the daily path,
Burning for those men filled with wrath.

5 A.M.

To feel alive before the sun
And sit in solemn contemplation,
Broken only by a peaceful voice
Now nesting in your ears,
Making you nostalgic
For a life you never knew;
And sip a cup of steamy tea
Freshly brewed as the morning dew,
Feeling like a warm embrace
From the dark itself,
Caressing your insides,
And makes you feel excited just to be alive.
That divine humanity
Found only in pure solitude,
Thriving in the sublime morn,
Giving you the strength
To face the coming day
You warmly invite.

A Spiral Stair

Twisting, turning, crawling, creeping
Through this labyrinthine prison,
Ever wandering, wondering, wishing
To see the sun that shines on me
And warms my skin but evades my gaze
As my neck fails to turn and stretch
My limbs trapped at my side,
Losing feeling, growing numb
My soul sleeps in my feet
Forever wanting to awake
And laugh, cry, scream
At a god that forgot it's creation
Now walking, running, sprinting
Tripping on its own feet
Falling always down, consumed
In the heat of a stairwell
No other man has climbed.
The empty hall extends onward,
Never twisting, changing, always growing
Below me with no end now except for
Death, collapsing to the floor,
Claiming the body, the soul as well
But the will of the man stands up
And singing, dancing, shouting
At a boss, at a god,

"I don't care. Terminate my presence here
While I dance amongst these spinning lights
Above my head that aren't the sun
Because they give no warmth
And because I can see them.
Remove me from this enclosed place,
This hall, this room, this stair
In which I wither away,
Growing weaker, working harder
All alone with faces that don't hear,
Don't respond, with whom I laugh
At an unheard joke."
The man now thinks he leaves the place,
Body and soul still in the stair
Ascending upward, downward
Yet no left or right to free the man
Who climbs and climbs but will never see the
top,
The climax of a laugh at a joke
The man doesn't know but lived
Buried in for his whole life
In the labyrinthine prison of
Walls, halls, sun-like lights
That are not suns, but the man thinks they are
When his soul dies dancing
Forever wandering, wondering, wishing
To escape the place with no doors or windows
Through which he can walk, run, sprint
But instead trip on his own feet

That take him back to the beginning he forgot
Who I am, who travels through this place
As him, with body and soul severed
That wither, die together, die apart
Having forgot the desperate cries
Of a dying man at an absent god
Dead from the start, no hope for them, for us,
Twisting, turning, crawling, creeping
Through this labyrinthine prison.

To Zosima

You, in your wise old years, say that
"All of life is paradise,"
And how I wish I could agree
But when I look around me
All I see is misery.
Perhaps life was better
Back in your day and age
But in this world that we've now made
I face only men depraved,
Whose capacity to love
Is replaced with brutal fear
And who think they make the grandest art
By destroying all that they hold dear.
Oh but how I wish that like yourself
I could look upon the sun and sky
And see within it the whole of life
And hear "Hosanna" from my tongue cry
At being blessed to have bestowed
All of God's beloved beauty
On my soul deep in the mines,
But when I look down again
Upon the road there is only a dying dog
His body cut in half
His head bucking up shouting for help
That now could not mend

His innocent body abandoned there
To suffer for one man's sin.
And if I could just sit and stare
Upon the glorious sky
I would,
But that does not change
The dying dog still at my feet,
For the Devil has not yet sang to God
His miraculous "Hosanna"
So still I must look down and act
Just as all men do.
And you, great elder, just sit and watch all day,
But I do not see how you can live
Locked away inside those walls
And only eat and pray,
Knowing what horror lies just outside.
Despite that though you still proudly say
That "all of life is paradise."
Well is it so for those of us
Outside your sacred walls
Or are we forever cursed to wander life's empty
halls
In search of a paradise we cannot find
Upon this wretched Earth?
For am I blessed to have watched
That dog die helplessly
Or does the beauty lie in his memory
Realized only here and now
As I sit and hear the leaves of the trees

Rustle in the wind
And feel the sun warm my skin
And taste the summer air
And think about that poor dog
Lying dead in the street
Who knows this calmness no more now
And for whom I uselessly weep.
Was there beauty in his death itself
Or does it exist only now
That he was blessed enough not to die alone
And is turned to simple words
That were not here before
On this empty page
Because the one who saw him pass
Could make art out of his death
That honored him, that nameless dog,
In his final breath.
Yet such atrocities occur
Without any one to see
And within their gruesome depths
Recover their true beauty
And I simply do not understand
How all of that can justify
The art made by one hand,
Remembering only one such death
Caused by one horrid man.
Or does Hosanna lie in these lines
Crying out to Him in His gracious mercy
For those unknown

When experiencing their demise.
Shouting for their peace
No longer on this Earth,
Do these artful lines
That contain a glimpse of beauty
Fix the wrongs that have been done
Just because men act?
And I think I say
All of the right things
But I still don't see how they are true
So you, great elder, enlighten me,
I beg of you,
So I can see how I am right
To make beauty out of death.
Please show me the truest light
So I can justify
The countless deaths of nameless dogs
And so I can sing out to Him
My purest "Hosanna".

Disillusionment

Again, I sit, I sit and think
And wade to deep
And wait to dream
And be elsewhere
Somewhere else, deep
Inside my mind, that sinks.

On the brink, destruction waits
And stalks and taunts
With that which seems
To be, but is not there
And it still haunts
And seals my fate.

Again, I sit, I sit and dream of things that cannot
be
And wish that I could be elsewhere, some place
where I am free.

A Parking Lot Funeral

The room is unbearably cold from the blast of
the fans.
At least the plant is real.
It's being fake would prove a cruel irony in this
place.
The waiting feels like the room itself,
Unbearably cold.
Outside, away from this place is warm
But it reeks of oil and dirt.
We are taken to an empty room,
Filled with man's last sanctuary.
The walls are pure white, the lights blindingly
fluorescent.
In that place they must be, lest you take in the
full sight before your eyes.
Tear drops hit the floor, the scratchy blanket, the
rubber skin.
There is no comfort in that place.
There, one must face nature as it is.
I said I wouldn't cry, but there you cannot help
yourself.
You cannot help but indulge in humanity.
At least the lights are blinding.
The fish are insultingly bright, the only color in
that place.

They remind me I need water before I suffocate
on air.
How can something live in such a place, and be
forever clueless?
How can they never know this feeling?
I hate the vibrant fish, and envy them all the
same.
They can be comfortable here,
A feeling I cannot yet know,
Even in a room of pews for a god I do not feel
here
Though somewhere here He must be.
It's dark, and quiet, and entirely empty.
There are hundreds of crosses on the walls,
But not a single one comes for me.
None helps in the way whispered notes to a
wishful song has.
"Weep no more. Dry your eyes."
But with what can I do so?
With useless tissues, on a useless pew?
The air outside evaporates the tears.
Help comes for me there.
A desert of weathered lines on cracked asphalt,
Where I can be alone before the mindless eyes
of passers-by
And pray to the god who was distant from those
pews and crosses,
Befriend the rocks that hit the truck as my feet
pace through that place.

I hope for a sign, a spirit, Angel, even demon,
Whose presence alone will make this verse as
transcendent as it feels.
But nobody watches from the curbs, beyond the
chain-link fence
That confines me to this hell.
And that is alright, because at least I have the
barking dogs
And the beating sun, that warms my frozen skin,
And the breeze that fills my lungs with horrid oil
and dirt,
And brings more comfort than those walls.
At least here I can sit, and feel, and laugh, and
cry.
At least here I can sing, and scream, and
whimper
All alone before the eyes of those who do not
watch,
Those who will not question me
As I wander through that forgotten place
Seen only by a god in a burnt sky, whose eyes I
do not meet
As I take comfort in the rocks and trash below
my feet.
In this place, all of life can happen in an instant.
It sees all things from below, content, knowing
that it lays forgotten,
Feeding itself on the souls who go there without
comfort

And to them it gives life.
Soon, I too will leave behind this oasis
But I will remember the water it gave to me,
A water more refreshing than that of the fish
inside.
I will remember the life it placed in my reluctant
hand
And the heaven that desert built from sand.
All things return to the place with no parking
lots.
Where then shall we receive comfort amidst the
darkest depths of grief?

In Memory of Lost Times

To look into thine eyes is to grieve
And lament in memory of the times
Lost long ago when you had to leave
As I sat and listened to church bells chime.
Wishing to see that smile again
That has faded from thy crimson lips.
Tis a sorrowful effort done in vain
To preserve thy beauty as harsh Fate snips.
Oh how cruel it is to see thee sleep,
While, for your beauty, I must weep!

Ode to The Neglected Memorial

The air is sour, stale, and sickly,
Sweetly singing with a static hum
I do not hear as I listen weakly
To a voice ready to succumb
To the depths of despair found in that place
Deathly silent and deadly still
Whose air or rotting wood tastes
And suffocates in a haunting chill
Forgotten in this mindless maze
Of blaring music and dead-end shops
That numb the thoughts in a hard-hearted haze,
But not her voice that shouts, "Does it ever stop,
The death and deception remembered there
And there alone for here it's gone
Except to us who care and share
In their complacency none."
And in that way I still remain
In immense grief, hunched on that bench
Hearing the voices who lived that pain
And dig within my mind a trench
I cannot climb, in spite of distractions much,
Of food and friends and games,
Whose joyous spirit curses me such
To play and tolerate the voice that claims

That all is well despite my absent mind
Still trapped within that rotting wood
The greater good of which I cannot find
If, to its horror, all are blind.

Tapping

I heard a tap out in the hall.
Tap… tap… tap… it went along the porcelain
floor.
Each coming closer in a steady time,
Until I heard the final tap just outside my door.

I hid my head below the sheets
Not wanting to see
The thing now tapping at the wood
Wishing to gain entry.

In the door there stood the thing
Pale and sickly, tall and lean
With thin hair of spiders black as night
And piercing eyes with bloodshot sheen.

A grating sound came from the thing,
And from its mouth these words did seep,
"Little boy, I know you're there and wide awake,
Lying there and feigning sleep.

"Don't you think that you can hide,
I always catch my prey,
Though for tonight, lay in peace
Since here is where I'll stay."
And so it did, for the whole night

Not moving from its spot,
Simply standing, tapping on
Leaving petrified me to rot.

I heard the tap again tonight.
Tap…tap… through the silent sleeping house
Soon to reach my bedroom door
Now squeaking like a mouse.

"You didn't think I was a dream
Did you, little boy?
Well here I am again tonight
For your fear, which I'll enjoy."

And the tapping grew louder still
Louder, louder, across the floor
Until the terror loomed over me
Watching, tapping, tapping more.

"I'll take you soon but not tonight,
So there's no need to cower still.
Rest, my child, dream, dream on
Because soon I'll get my fill."

Just like this it watches me
Each and every night
Simply tapping, on and on
Filling me with fright.

Until one night the tapping stopped
And I thought I had been saved.
Great relief washed over me
To not see the thing, depraved.

So I turned over in my bed
Ready to rest well,
But in my bed there was the thing
So close that I could smell.

"Hello, my boy, why so afraid?
Are you shocked to see me here?
Just because I did not tap
Doesn't mean I can't appear."

Now the thing, it taps no more
And I don't know where it will be.
It says my time has all run out
But my end I don't foresee.

And no more I sleep within the night
Until, in the morning, I must arise.
Though I think it only waits for me
To, in my fear, bring my demise.

Campaigning

To stand in no man's land is to die,
To entrust yourself to that merciless god,
Death himself, and to sacrifice your soul
For no apparent cause.
In that land of sunken ground
On the precipice of life and death,
Though no life is to be found
Befitting of a man,
Resounding cries and shouts surround
From both parties opposed in mortal strife
But depend on each other for meaning and life;
On every side, a beckoning call,
But you know not to trust their empty pleas
Because no safer are you there than here
So here you stay on unsteady feet
Resolved to stay right where you fall,
A vote of no confidence,
And watch the bullets fly
And darken the bright blue sky.
And there you watch the souls of many
Fall into the dirt and dust
All for a cause as old as time
And for which I only breathe a hopeless sigh.

What the Animals Knew

In the beginning, when the Earth was young
And it was full of light and hope
From its earth all of life sprung
And God willed that man awoke.

And God said unto His son
"Look upon this world I've made,
Your power over which has just begun
And it will all obey you, if only I'm obeyed".

And man looked upon the Earth
And listened to Him for some time
Until one day a serpent gave birth
To thoughts of sin within his mind.

And from The Tree, an Apple he took
So he could be equal to his God
But when he, at himself looked
He saw he was equal only to the sod.

So man left behind this fruitful place
And tried to justify himself
By forgetting his God that he would replace
With creations from his mind itself.

And the animals saw all that man could do
And at first trembled with fear.
But after little time they knew
That man would soon disappear.

For the deer saw man chase them down
Not with their bare hands
But with weapons they had found
Just to drive them from their lands.

And the fish watched as man would hunt
With contraptions made of string
All to trap them from the front
So that they could eat and sing.

And the horses watched as man rejected their
own feet
And instead created carts and wheels
And the horses they would beat
Until they conformed to their ideals.

And men were watched even by the bears
Who were content in their quaint caves
That did not satiate the men who dare
To turn the very trees into their slaves.

And the whales and sea critters saw
Man build great tanks of steel
To traverse the ocean with no law

And would, his precious life, steal.

And the birds watched men build wings below
So that he could also fly
Though too close to the sun they would go
Just to once touch the foreign sky.

And the sly fox watched men as well
And saw the treachery he could bring
That would forcefully end with death's bell
That seemed to daily cruelly ring.

And the vicious lion saw murder in the streets
And gaped at man's immense cowardice
And the deception in his feats
That left his fellow creatures powerless.

And every animal came together to watch the
men
Gather opposed in fearsome troupes
And charge at each other again and again
Until all fell upon the ground in the warring
groups.

And the animals watched as man
Never made peace amongst themselves
Because they refused His great plan
So they could subdue all of creation themselves.

For man did not trust
Nature, made distant from his life,
But chose instead to return to the dust
Filled with unnatural strife.

And this is what the animals knew-
The many horrors man could devise.
For always the mind, man's greatest gift, grew
Guaranteeing his own demise.

The Woods

What brings you into these woods
Of twisted trees and bleary branches?
Did you mean to wander here in search of goods
To like me find only harsh scratches
From those limbs that promised me
Warmth and comfort in their embrace?
What do you think you will be
Once you brave this perilous place?
Well, let me tell you what you will find
If you undertake this lonesome trek.
Upon you will be placed the curse of the
philosopher's mind
To crane up and down your neck
But never to look straight ahead
And enjoy life's simplicity.
A great sand dune will fill your head
That you will climb for eternity
While you will endlessly agonize
Over the width of each and every grain
And in the end you will be wise
And, despite feeling entrapped in chains,
More than most men you will be free.
More than your fill you will drink
But at the bottom you will find the key

To life's happiness if only you are willing to
sink.
That's what waits for you in these woodlands
If you can persevere this winding path
And fulfill the forest's many demands
And not develop for it great wrath.
And in the end you will be happy
If you can withstand the mind's immense
misery.

The Traveller

"Beware the lonely traveller," they often say,
"For he may try to tempt with frivolous delights,
Valueless, he will do with you what he may
And to you show such unholy sights."

Walking down a dark and empty road,
Between the rows of strong and mighty oaks,
I search in vain for hope's abode,
Looking to that bark for help as they awoke.

At this time the first of many guests appears.
A young man whose face content, seems to
glow.
I ask the stranger, "What great fortune does
befall thee, if I may hear?"
To which he says, "My friend, you know me not
for my days are never low.
And wherever I may go fortune shall follow
close behind.
Never in my time have I known sorrow, grief, or
fear.
Let me say this my desperate friend-Join me and
you will find
The same fortunes in your life. If this tempts
you, let our union be so."

Behind this young man's eyes I could see
passion burning violently
So though I envied his fortune much, I knew his
promise would never truly be.

Further down the shadowed road, the silent day
begins to wane
When, faint, I hear the sound of clanking metal.
A grandiose man approaches me, who from his
pockets golden coins rain.
I say to him, "Good sir, don't you wish to hide
your wealth, lest on your neck a knife may
settle?"
Rather proudly he responds "If such a day
comes I will give what the dagger seeks.
But, my poor, poor friend, you yourself seem to
be bound in poverty's chain.
Why don't you take this shining silver and
deliver my spoken fate?"
And in my hand a blade did rest, but already I
know that in his affairs I should not meddle.
The hushed forest is only interrupted now by a
warm and gentle thud.
For though my soul is plagued by poverty, my
avarice should not begin to bud.

The sky is colored a deep red behind the trees
black as night

When I am again left to my woe and anger starts
to grow.
Absorbed by audacious emotion, I am blinded to
the dark figure within my sight.
The humanoid shape comes close to me
speaking these words deep and slow:
"I see that your shadow becomes a vicious
cloud. Do you not
Doubt your virtue? Do you not begin to wonder
if you might
To heaven go? Let me ask, revenge have you not
yet sought?"
That man that I hated so, the dark figure to me
shows.
And then behind my evil eye, odious images
start to play
But despite my boundless power, I, basked in
red light, fall to my knees and pray.

The being before me disappears with my final
violent 'amen'.
The world around me, shrouded in darkness, felt
all the more oppressive now.
I continue down the pitch black path only
broken by moonlight now and then,
When in the distance a yellow light pierces the
night, and I hope for refuge if the glow allows.
A small, comfortable home greets me there and
from its door

A woman emerges and invites me in saying, "I
don't get visitors very often.
Here, have a seat. Can I bring you anything?
How long have you been walking for?"
My host treats me kindly as I rest my weary
body until to me she says this vow:
"Stay here away from that treacherous road and
forget your misery so long as you may live,"
And with those words my mind was moved that
to her my idleness I could not give.

The moon now sits high in the sky, watching as I
stumble down the road.
I dare not let my famished body sit for fear that I
may never again stand.
I walk without direction until I find a field where
the seeds of sin are sowed
And wait for me as an overflowing table with a
feast and man who holds in his hand
A chalice filled with wine. He says to me,
"Good sir, I congratulate you for now your
journey ends
And you may rest and celebrate with food and
drink until your troubled mind has slowed.
My friend, indulge in your delights and know
that here you will no-one offend."
Ready I was to sit and drink my fill when in my
palm my cup crumbled into sand.

Ready I had been to drink myself to drunkenness
and abandon my cause entirely.
Ready I had been to indulge in sin and forget my
virtues completely.

I return to my desolate road with a feeling of
abandonment.
My soul, once lost to horrid passion, now feels
empty and emotionless.
The moon watches from behind as I hope for an
end to my torment
When, seemingly all around a calliope voice
speaks soft words that do caress
My whole being. "Do not stress anymore, my
sweet. Come and let me hold you tight
So you may forget your sorrow and tomorrow
awake having forsaken this pitiful descent.
Come with me and you may see the pleasures of
the flesh on this fateful night."
In vain I hunt the source of this Siren song
longing for fulfillment of my soul left
passionless.
She whispers sweet seductions all throughout
the night promising her warming love
But when morning comes my barren bones lay
in the dust and she leaves like a startled dove.

The road is now far from my sight as the sun
scorches the heavens and the Earth.

My body and soul, too weak to walk, remain in
the arid dirt as soft footsteps approach.
The man before me begins to speak and I can
quickly see that though he is of unholy birth,
He has come for me. "Here you rest amongst the
muck as nothing more than a roach.
In spite of your ornate morals you, like all men,
fall to sweet, sinful desires.
Here you rest having failed the truest test of
moral men, unveiling your real worth
As equal to the dirt. Like the rest in times of
torment the smallest spark fills you with fire
Burning ardently. You are not what you say.
Your actions bring unto your soul great reproach
That no prayer will mend. Chasing light you
claim to be a holy man but now I'm sure you see
That The Prince of Darkness comes for you and
you must come with me."

"Beware the lonely traveller," they often say,
"For he may try to tempt with frivolous delights,
Valueless, he will do with you what he may
And to you show such unholy sights."

Take The Hand Before Your Eye

Take the hand before your eye,
For who's to say if it will stay
And be there when you die
Or leave you alone in the filthy clay.

Take the hand upon your cheek
And hold it to you tight,
For unto you it may pity and speak,
"Let us reach for the light."

The Patron of the Coffeehouse in the Evening

A lonely patron drinks at a bar,
Searching for his love in the night sky,
For, to them, the distance seems that far,
But his vision is obscured by the lamplight in his
eye
So he returns to the dark figures around,
In high spirits and joyous company,
But in his ears only his pain resounds
And he cannot help but long drunkenly
For a time when he savored love's sweet
embrace,
Not long ago, but a finite infinity
When, instead of weeping, he would revel in this
place
With his light, his guiding star, to show the way
Through the void, weighing down upon his
head,
Now a mere forgotten dream, fleeing with the
come of day
And abandoning him to an empty bed,
Where he tries to remember his Sweet's honeyed
love,
That gentle kind so natural to them
And makes his soul flutter like the calming dove

Until his deathly eyes begin to dim
And he dreams of fruitful meadows far away
Where he and his love can happily forever stay.

The Sandstorm

I never learned to ride a bike.
Where was there for me to go
In this convoluted concrete jungle?
What was there outside these walls,
A supposed refuge from the storm outside,
The calm and grounding eye
At the center of the raging tempest,
Beyond acidic air that scorched the lungs
And caked corruption to the skin?
There, only foul fear pervades the air
To fill desperate men with deep despair.
But still I longed for that profound love
In the poems and stories of old
That brought hope to hopeless men,
Though there it wasn't to be found
Except in novels of another time.
But if you travel behind the sandstorm
You will find a sympathetic oasis,
Waiting for the lost who wander far into the
desert.
There, among those mighty trees,
That played the music of the wind
As it danced across its varied leaves,
That raised my head up to the sun
And compelled me to turn to the night sky,

Where a thousand glorious worlds
I never knew were there, prevailed
And in that luscious lake
Of pure refreshing water,
The substance of life itself
That enfolds you in a cool embrace
And revives the withered body,
Clinging onto life with acrid drink
There I found that glorious love
I had abandoned long ago,
And there I learned again
To love and trust my fellow man
And exalt in life's simplicity.
It was there in God's greatest creation
I was taught that this is how men are meant to
be.

The Oasis

Oh, there is a blessing in this calm zephyr,
That complete stillness found in warm nights
In early fall, when the leaves threaten change-
An utter lack of movement in the air
That brings peace where there was none before
And refreshing rest unto a weary soul.
Where the breeze has gone I neither know nor
care,
For now I only revel in my brief reprieve
From the constant noise that followed me
before,
Before this scarcity of life. I breathe again!
The pure unfiltered air floods life into my lungs
And I feel myself unburdened of my former
course,
A way that could never know humanity
And deprived men of his dazzling divinity.
But here men become drunk on non-existence
And can learn what it means to simply be
And discover how to enjoy one's own company.
Oh, Beautiful Liberty in endless possibility
Tainted with no necessity to act
But welcomes willing action all the same
Except for in this passing moment
In which the only proper sensation

Is that I cannot feel the air surrounding me.
And in that fleeting void I can rediscover
My hope for all this loving life can bring.